Inside London
Photographs by Dorothy Bohm

Inside London

Photographs by Dorothy Bohm
Words by Jessica Duchen
Foreword and picture selection by Martin Harrison

Lund Humphries
in association with
The Photographers' Gallery, London

First published in 2000 by
Lund Humphries
Gower House
Croft Road
Aldershot
Hampshire GU11 3HR

in association with
The Photographers' Gallery
5 Great Newport Street
London WC2H 7HY

Lund Humphries is part of Ashgate Publishing

Inside London: Photographs by Dorothy Bohm © 2000
The Photographers' Gallery
Photographs by Dorothy Bohm © 2000 the photographer
Texts © 2000 the authors

British Library Cataloguing-in-Publication Data
A catalogue record for this book is available from
the British Library

ISBN 0 85331 780 1

Designed by Martin Harrison
Printed in Great Britain by
BAS Printers, Over Wallop, Hampshire

Ashgate US office:
Ashgate Publishing Company
131 Main Street
Burlington
VT 05401
USA

Distributed to the book trade in North America by
Antique Collectors' Club
Market Street Industrial Park
Wappingers Falls
NY 12590
USA

11

Blackfriars Bridge
16.05.98

Bow
13.07.98

Clerkenwell
18.07.98

14

Inside London
by Jessica Duchen

A cusp is time and place in the making. Nothing is what it seems; the past is fading, but the future remains veiled. In this moment, unseen beneath a silent, silken surface, works the process of metamorphosis in which new energy mysteriously erupts into being, layered, translucent and luminous. The transition period from an old century into a new is such a cusp. Under its folded wings seethe the colours that could at any moment explode dazzlingly into a fresh era, in a place where everything is in constant, frenetic motion and transformation. This is the time. The place is London.

London! What is London? London is what you make it. No two Londoners will ever have the same perception of their city, for perception depends on personal attitude. In London you can rejoice at the richness of culture, the cornucopia of shops, food, theatre or beer. You can relish the multicultural diversity of the city, where anyone and anything goes. Or else you can despair at the marked contrasts between the wealthiest regions and the most poverty stricken, often existing cheek by jowl upon one another's doorsteps.

Islington
23.09.98

You can walk through the streets and spot the fascinating details of architecture, notice the way nature creeps in, encroaching on urbanisation in a frail, struggling tree trunk or the reflection of passing clouds in a plate glass window. Or else you can see only the endlessly clogged traffic, the crumbling public transport, the fumes, the stress, the road rage.

Whatever you see, a few years ago it was not quite the same; and in a few years' time it will have changed again. London has always improvised itself. As in the improvisation of modern jazz, nothing that emerges is expected, nothing is at once purely coherent, nothing precisely repeats itself: variations on a theme.

What is the theme? Could it be greyness? London's greyness is fabled, and if you look for greyness, you will see it, even though the smogs are gone; there are still grey skies, grey streets, grey roofs, grey concrete department stores in Oxford Street, grey stone lions in Trafalgar Square. Yet this grey, heavy city is splashed over and over with colour, like a canvas painted with a bizarre mix of oils and pastels and watercolours, around which the artist has hinted at a border of grey, to remind you of what might have been…

I grew up in north-west London and have lived in the city all my life. But while I was growing up in London, London was growing up around me. As adolescent trauma hit me, back in the late 1970s, the city I'd spent my childhood adoring seemed to be crumbling around me. Split into a mess of independent boroughs, the city's unity was shattered. Nothing could quite hold it together; buildings and bridges were neglected (except for the Houses of Parliament, washed down and restored), and the increasing numbers of homeless people adopted streets, subways and shop doorways as their only hope. Litter blew in the wind, the underground broke down and friendly bus conductors lost their jobs. The city was vast and grey, broken-hearted.

Perhaps the prospect of an impending new century was the best thing that ever happened to London. No awareness-raising campaign could have done a better job at convincing the demoralised populace that their city had to be overhauled extensively to become a thoroughly modern metropolis. That awareness coincided fortuitously with a soaring economy in which public, private and National Lottery money began to be directed into the regeneration of the UK's capital city. As time slid closer to the end of the twentieth century, I walked along the pavements I knew so well and experienced a new sensation. London was buzzing.

Royal Festival Hall
South Bank
28.03.97

There was building everywhere: cranes, skips, scaffolding. The Jubilee Line extension opened (if late) and suddenly the east of the city, with its ambitious riverside developments, was finally accessible with ease. Great booms rang out across the river near Charing Cross as the foundations were laid for a new footbridge. People who had never taken an interest in politics became passionate and involved as a referendum declared that London would finally have its own mayor with an elected authority overseeing the city as a whole – even if the contest that followed was perhaps less inspiring...

Meanwhile, the film industry began to boom. Art of all types filled every gallery, from the finest photography to the ever-controversial Turner Prize. The conversion of a disused power station into the vast Tate Modern gallery was underway. Music flourished everywhere – live jazz bands performed in restaurants and bars, folk music from every corner of the globe blossomed under the new 'World Music' banner, and the Royal Opera House rose (amid much controversy) from its Victorian gloom to become the most advanced state-of-the-art opera house in Europe. Youngsters from all over the world flocked into the clubs and the new cafés and declared London the coolest city of the continent.

Best of all, for caffeine addicts like me, you can at long last get a decent cup of coffee anywhere in London – in fact, you'd be hard-pressed to avoid it. Strangely enough, just as Italy and Spain and Denmark were gleefully opening pubs, Londoners were discovering the joys of cafés (see pp.52-3 or p.55). Now the city is full of pleasant, lively places to eat mozzarella, tomato and basil ciabatta and drink 'skinny lattes', read the paper, talk to friends and watch the world go by without the smell of stale beer and crisps and the noise of Space Invader machines! Why did it take so long, we wonder, sipping contentedly?

Upper Street
Islington
21.09.98

21

Kentish Town
28.08.97

23

Camden High Street
28.08.97

Who are 'we'? We are Londoners – and we are anyone and everyone, from anywhere, of any age. London is home to both the richest and the poorest people in the UK, the most comfortable and the most desperately deprived. Being a Londoner can be a difficult, divisive, guilt-ridden and stressful way of life. Yet probably the largest number of Londoners love this variety too, precisely because it leaves us no room for complacency.

London's thirty-something women, like me and my friends and colleagues, have a special tightrope to tread: to us falls the apparently impossible management of marriage and family in combination with time-consuming commuting to busy jobs and/or demanding careers. We are well aware that we're the first generation to grow up not only knowing we can 'have it all', but expecting to 'have it all' as our birthright as London women. We respect ourselves. The anarchistic Punk movement with its Mohican hair and cult of ugliness – the rebellious, adolescent phase, perhaps, of modern London – has virtually disappeared. The city has reached adulthood and we, embracing our best years, have found dignity as well as femininity and developed our confidence, perhaps for the first time. You will see some of that confidence reflected in these photographs.

Our hair is long and flowing, or cropped stylishly at some expense. We wear anything we like. Our skirts are very short or very long, but mostly we wear trousers. We can don jeans – designer or Marks and Spencer – and leather jackets or cotton shirts or bright fleeces. We diet. We exercise. The men still wolf-whistle at us from building sites, but we don't give a damn any more (see pp.22-3). Perhaps men generally are more humble than they used to be, mellowed by active fatherhood or sobered by the demise of the notion of a job for life. They exercise too, however. We all have to look after ourselves, male and female, young and old, because in London we know we can do anything and be anything, but only through our own efforts. Nobody can ever help us but ourselves.

As we set out into a world in which the possibilities are greater but the globe smaller than ever before, we improvise our own existences, as our city does around us. We're cosmopolitan. We have little in common with the rest of England, but neither are we quite European – yet. We love city life, but sometimes we hate it too.

Often we have to struggle. Jobs aren't as secure as they once were. Crazy house prices drive us to live further and further away from the city centre. Journeys grow slower and more expensive on ever more congested roads and railways. And we panic about where our children will be schooled even before we have any. We work the longest hours in Europe. We go to our offices, pressed into tube trains in conditions of heat, cramp and airlessness that would spark virulent protests by animal rights activists if foisted upon poor defenceless cattle. Who knows why we put up with it?

Greenwich
14.12.97

Roman Road
Bethnal Green
06.07.97

But we're all in it together, black and white and brown, immigrant or Anglo-Saxon, first generation British or hundredth. Just as this city grew without any coherent system – a gaggle of villages and developments of all eras that simply melded together over time – we encounter one another by chance and explore one another's worlds, almost unawares, on a daily basis. We know nothing of the strangers in the street, or the man whose heavy foot crushes our toes on the Piccadilly Line – yet behind every pair of eyes there is a unique story and a unique soul.

And if you set out to look for the soul of London, there is only one place you will find it: in its people. If you want to see London, look into the eyes of the young girl selling *The Big Issue*, or the woman immersed in the *News of the World* at Whitechapel market (p.35), or the young father buying a snack for his child at the Moscow State Circus (p.41). The human spirit, with all its extraordinary resources and resilience, is the only constant in the changing world.

There's still squalor in London – there always was and there always will be. But somehow, today there is a spring in the city's step alongside that squalor. It's easier, amid the fluidity of change, the new organic soup take-aways, the sprouting Internet cafés, the American bookstores, to notice the details that transform our view of this city.

Hampstead High Street
09.07.97

Look up and you might be surprised by what you see. Your perspective shifts. Sometimes that perspective turns surreal: on posters, huge faces or flat paper dogs the size of small dinosaurs dwarf the shoppers and workers on the pavement below (pp.36-7). Mouldings on buildings, shop signs, balconies bearing plants and washing and sometimes much stranger objects too, rise out as if taking to the sky. You seem to be walking through one vast Chagall canvas, complete with giant flying animals.

Something as ordinary as a skip beside a building site can suddenly become beautiful when the light changes. Graffiti looms ghostlike out of walls and street signs, burying identities. The specific becomes abstract, the abstract becomes personal. The perception of an object, a glimpsed expression, a passing sound or a sliver of sky is the same from no two angles and at no two moments. Everything is interesting, and every object or every place, as well as every person, has a story to tell.

Many of the old traditions survive: London's buses are still red (some are, anyway), the taxis are still (mostly) black, and small boys wear ties with their school uniforms even if their fathers go to work in jeans and trainers. The tourist attractions – Buckingham Palace, Madame Tussaud's, the Tower of London, Westminster Abbey – still attract tourists. London has always been a Mecca to performing artists of all types, and it still is – from the Moscow State Circus to concert pianists and famous orchestras at the Proms, from Hollywood actors dreaming of the fabled West End theatres to pop bands dreaming of Wembley Arena.

But alongside these time-honoured, memory-loaded monuments and traditions, London has been learning to tell a different story, and to swing to a different melody accompanied by compelling new rhythms. Now you are as likely to hear salsa drifting from a bar as the Spice Girls, and as likely to notice a Peruvian folk band or a Chinese flute player busking in Covent Garden as a clarinettist or fiddler. One of my favourite sound symbols of multicultural London was a solitary Jamaican steel drummer beside Hungerford Bridge – playing the Hebrew song 'Hava nagila'.

London has become one of the most ethnically mixed cities in the world. Londoners are a colourful lot these days, and proud of it. Just look at the restaurants: Afro-Caribbean people eating Dim Sum, Asians eating bagels, English football fans putting away huge helpings of curry, Japanese businessmen tucking into pizza and pasta, young office girls enjoying fajitas and knocking back margaritas. Take a look at a newspaper stand and sometimes you will see more foreign language papers than English (see p.54).

Although there are inevitably pockets of racism and fear, the vast majority of London's multicoloured millions get along with one another perfectly well. Go to an evening class – and London has thousands of such classes, in everything from computing to car maintenance to meditation or feng shui – and the students' range of backgrounds are bound to be every bit as diverse as the range of subjects on offer. Our religions are infinite, varied or non-existent, but we have two things in common: we love to eat ice-cream even in cold weather; and when the sun comes out, we go outside and soak it up by the bucketful! Global warming or not, sun in London is still a precious and beloved commodity.

Whitechapel Road
Bethnal Green
19.10.97

What will emerge from this huge, seething chrysalis that is London today? London is inventing itself anew, but it is difficult to look far into the veiled future: the image on that photograph is as yet undeveloped. Perhaps the new Greater London Authority will transform the city into a united metropolis that takes pride in itself in every corner – or perhaps it won't. Perhaps the River Thames, which should be the core of the whole city, yet somehow is not, will regain its one-time centrality – but perhaps it won't.

Maybe cars will be banned from the city centre, bicycles and pedestrians encouraged and supported, access for disabled people improved on the underground and the buses – or maybe the jams and the fumes and the clashes between cyclists and taxi drivers will continue for another century. Who knows, perhaps one day the tube will be modernised too.

For the first time in decades it is tempting to be optimistic, yet few Londoners dare to believe the best; whatever happens, things are unlikely to grow easier. London life has never been easy and it never will be – exciting, yes, but easy, no. London is a high-maintenance life-partner: it has much to give, but it demands just as much in return.

Perhaps we will carry on improvising, as we always have. Perhaps what we can enjoy most are the unexpected juxtapositions created by our improvisation, the modern jazz that is London life, created by every individual in counterpoint to every other individual, each with a new interplay of circles and threads, colours and light, major and minor, piano and drums. Perhaps it's chaos – but as in chaos theory, patterns do emerge, patterns that are unplanned and unexplainable, mysterious and seductive, beautiful and abstract, obeying perhaps some inner law beyond our comprehension.

31

Whitechapel
19.10.97

Pilgrim's Lane
Hampstead
09.08.95

32

Whatever happens, we're moving on; beyond the struggles, there's a new century on the way, a blank sheet of photographic paper on which we can begin to capture the developing image of the future. In London, we can choreograph the dance of our own lives in our own streets, if we choose to do so. London, like all the world, is a stage where we play out our own infinitely numbered interactive dramas, as centuries of people have before us, and as generations after us always will.

Waterloo Station
01.10.97

Still Life With Theatre
Programme
16.01.99

Sunday Market
Whitechapel
19.10.97

Oxford Street
03.09.97

Young Vic Theatre Café
The Cut
01.10.97

39

Soho
01.02.98

Millie's Cookies
Victoria Station
08.03.92

41

During The Interval
Moscow State Circus
Crystal Palace
20.05.95

42

Covent Garden
20.12.97

43

Sunday Market
Camden Town
23.12.95

Spitalfields Market
28.07.97

46

Tottenham Court Road
18.10.97

Hampstead High Street
29.10.95

48

Gerard Street
Soho
05.10.95

The Mall
St James's
09.03.98

Torrens Street
Islington
21.01.99

53

Camden Town
25.01.97

Near The Angel
Islington
01.11.95

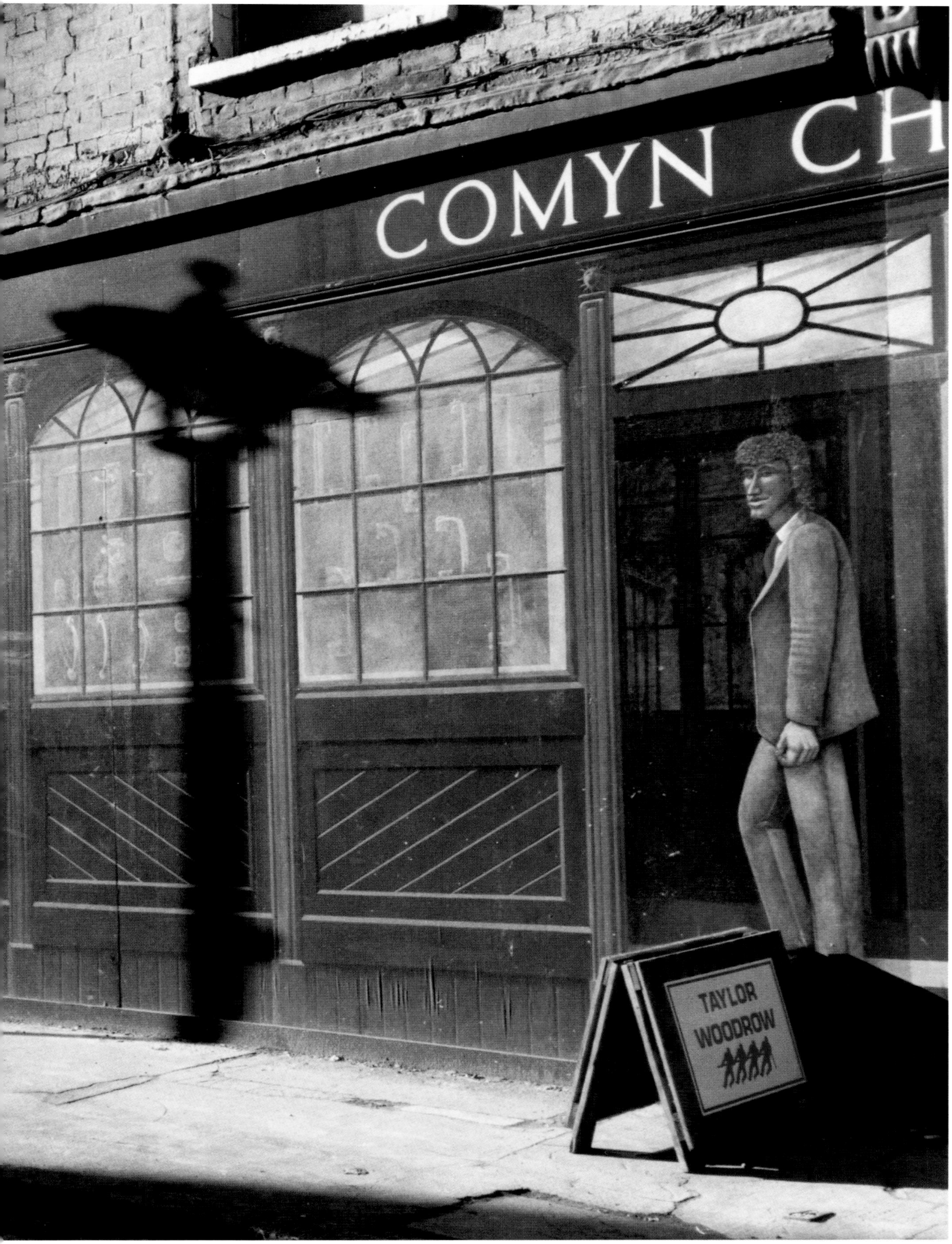

59

Shelton Street
Covent Garden
24.01.90

Hampstead
01.05.95

New Globe Theatre
South Bank
13.09.97

Kensington
19.10.97

65

66

New Contemporaries
Camden Arts Centre
09.09.97

South Bank
15.06.99

68

Art Fair
Duke of York's Barracks
King's Road, Chelsea
16.06.99

Past Gabriel's Wharf
South Bank
10.08.98

74

Bond Street
02.05.97

75

Stage Door
Cambridge Theatre
Covent Garden
29.01.98

Spitalfields Market
28.07.97

The Barbican
29.10.96

78

St John's Wood
09.09.97

Oxford Street
16.03.98

Waiting Area
Chelsea & Westminster
Hospital
Chelsea
15.06.99

Covent Garden
12.07.98

**From stairway leading
to Hayward Gallery
South Bank
15.06.99**

Pembridge Road
Notting Hill Gate
10.03.00

Moscow State Circus
Crystal Palace
20.05.95

Tottenham
05.07.97

90

Exmouth Market
18.07.98

Regent Street
20.04.96

Long Acre
Covent Garden
18.09.97

Whitecross Street
Moorgate
29.10.96

Earlham Street
16.03.96

96

St Gabriel's Wharf
South Bank
01.11.95

Spitalfields Market
28.07.97

98

St Pancras
22.01.98

Short Street
Southwark
01.10.97

106

Moscow State Circus
Crystal Palace
20.05.95

Barbican Centre
Music Shop
29.10.96

108

Christmas Fair
Leicester Square
23.12.95

Zippo's Circus
Hendon
19.10.97

110

Spitalfields Market
22.03.96

Oxford Street
16.03.98

112

**Gifts for Chinese
New Year
Soho
01.02.96**

113

Whitechapel Market
19.10.97

The taste that's stood the test of time
THE WORLD
CUP BAR!
RUGBY

taste that's stood the test of time

115

Covent Garden
10.07.98

Dorothy Bohm: Biography

1924 Born in Königsberg, East Prussia, of a Jewish Lithuanian family

1939 Arrived in England to finish her schooling at a girls' boarding school in Sussex

1942 Graduated from Manchester College of Technology and also obtained the City and Guilds Final Certificate in Photography

Worked in a leading portrait studio in central Manchester

1945 Married Louis Bohm

1946 Opened 'Studio Alexander' in Manchester

1952 Met Norman Hall at the Photokina in Cologne

1953 With her husband, who worked for a petrochemical company, moved to Paris

1956 Settled in Hampstead, North London

1957 Daughter Monica born

1958 Sold Manchester studio

1960 Daughter Yvonne born

1969 Participated in exhibition *Four Photographers in Contrast* (with Don McCullin, Tony Ray-Jones and Enzo Ragazzini), part of the photographic event 'Spectrum' at the Institute of Contemporary Arts

1970 First book of photographs published: *A World Observed*, with a Foreword by Roland Penrose

1971 The Photographers' Gallery was established by Sue Davies, assisted by Dorothy, who became Associate Director

1974 Travelled widely in South Africa

1975 Solo exhibition of photographs of London, Il Diaframma Gallery, Milan

1976 *Impressions of South Africa*, The Photographers' Gallery, London

1980 BBC Television documentary 'Dorothy Bohm – Photographer'

First experiments with colour photography

1981 Publication of *Hampstead – London Hill Town*

A Sense of Place, retrospective exhibition at Camden Arts Centre, London

1984 *A Celebration of London* published by André Deutsch

1986 Major retrospective at the Israel Museum, Jerusalem, curated by Nissan Perez, with a catalogue published by the Museum

1989 Participated with colour work in the international photography exhibition *City Lights* curated by Ian Jeffrey for Goldsmiths' College, London, which was subsequently toured by the South Bank Centre, London

Egypt, book of colour photography with a Foreword by Lawrence Durrell and an Afterword by Ian Jeffrey, published by Thames and Hudson

1992 Second book of colour photographs, *Venice*, published by Thames and Hudson

1994 Major retrospective exhibition of colour photography at The Photographers' Gallery, London, with a catalogue published by the Gallery

1995 In-depth interview with Mark Haworth-Booth for the Oral History of British Photography, National Sound Archive, British Library, London

1996 Publication of *Sixties London: Photographs* by Dorothy Bohm with texts by Amanda Hopkinson and Ian Jeffrey

1997 Exhibition of *Sixties London* at the Museum of London

1998 Solo exhibition of 125 new colour images entitled *Walls and Windows* at the Royal Photographic Society, Bath; subsequently shown at the Royal National Theatre, London

Book published by Lund Humphries of *Walls and Windows*, texts by Mark Haworth-Booth and Monica Bohm-Duchen

Still life colour photographs exhibited at Artmonsky Art Gallery in St John's Wood, London